DiscoverRoo
An Imprint of Pop!
popbooksonline.com

The Eras of Taylor Swift

THE LOVER era

1. I Forgot That You Existed
2. Cruel Summer
3. Lover
4. The Man
5. The Archer
6. I Think He Knows
7. Miss Americana & the Heartbreak Prince
8. Paper Rings
9. Cornelia Street
10. Death by a Thousand Cuts
11. London Boy
12. Soon You'll Get Better (ft. The Chicks)
13. False God
14. You Need to Calm Down
15. Afterglow
16. ME! (ft. Brendon Urie)
17. It's Nice to Have a Friend
18. Daylight

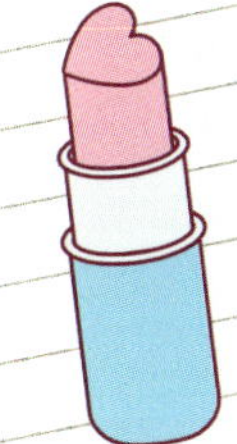

by Grace Hansen

WELCOME TO DiscoverRoo!

This book is filled with videos, puzzles, games, and more! Scan the QR codes* while you read, or visit the website below to make this book pop.

popbooksonline.com/Lover

abdobooks.com

Published by Pop!, a division of ABDO, PO Box 398166, Minneapolis, Minnesota 55439.

Printed in the United States of America, North Mankato, Minnesota.

082025
012026

Cover Photo: Alexandra Tarasova (BigArtLab); Shutterstock Images

Interior Photos: Charles Sykes/Invision/AP; Getty Images; Scott A Garfitt/Invision/AP; VICTOR AUBRY/SIPA/AP

Editors: Elizabeth Andrews and Anna Schwartz

Series Designer: Laura Graphenteen

Library of Congress Control Number: 2025941224

Publisher's Cataloging-in-Publication Data

Names: Hansen, Grace, author.

Title: The Lover era / by Grace Hansen

Description: Minneapolis, Minnesota : Pop!, 2026 | Series: The eras of Taylor Swift | Includes online resources and index

Identifiers: ISBN 9781098248710 (lib. bdg.) | ISBN 9781098249236 (ebook)

Subjects: LCSH: Swift, Taylor, 1989- --Juvenile literature. | Popular music--Juvenile literature. | Popular (Songs, etc.)--Juvenile literature. | Albums--Juvenile literature. | Concerts--Juvenile literature. | Mass media and music--Juvenile literature.

Classification: DDC 782.42164096--dc23

*Scanning QR codes requires a web-enabled smart device with a QR code reader app and a camera.

TABLE OF CONTENTS

CHAPTER 1

DAYLIGHT AFTER DARKNESS

Taylor Swift traveled for six months on her Reputation Stadium Tour. She said that the experience healed her in many ways. She felt like she could survive anything. Taylor also said her fans reminded her that she was "a flesh-and-blood human being." The version of her that the media had created was not real.

WATCH A VIDEO HERE!

Meet Taylor

Birthday: December 13, 1989
Star Sign: Sagittarius
Place of Birth: West Reading, PA
Favorite Number: 13
Favorite Color: Purple
Favorite Food: Chicken tenders and a chocolate shake
Meredith Grey
13
Benjamin Button
X O X O
Olivia Benson
Taylor Swift

Taylor used these realizations to write her seventh **studio** album. "This time around, I feel more comfortable being brave enough to be **vulnerable**," Taylor said.

On April 26, 2019, Taylor released the album's first **single**: "ME!" The catchy and upbeat tune featured the Panic! At The Disco frontman Brendon Urie.

Taylor's style was softer and more feminine in her Lover Era.

Urie and Swift first performed "ME!" live at the 2019 Billboard Music Awards.

On June 13, 2019, Taylor announced on an Instagram Live stream that her album *Lover* would **debut** in August. But first, she had a few more singles to share.

Taylor won Video of the Year at the 2019 MTV Video Music Awards for "You Need to Calm Down."

On June 14, "You Need to Calm Down" dropped. The song was Taylor's first big political statement. It addressed online hate and served as a message to those who spread negativity. Taylor asked people to be more accepting and to think before they said something unkind, especially toward certain groups of people who tend to be treated unfairly.

The album's title song, "Lover," was released on August 16. The three singles gave fans a good idea of the album as a whole. *Lover* would be **optimistic**, vulnerable, empowering, and, of course, focused on love.

Gibson created Lover *guitars for both the album's performances and Taylor's Eras Tour shows.*

Up until *Lover*, Taylor felt like she was always proving to others that she deserved to be where she was.

CHAPTER 2

A LOVE LETTER TO LOVE

After *Lover* was released on August 23, it became the best-selling album of 2019 in the United States. Globally, it was the best-selling album by a solo artist. Better yet, it seemed as if Taylor was everywhere promoting it.

EXPLORE LINKS HERE!

Some fans believe Taylor dyed her hair blue to represent her then-boyfriend Joe Alwyn's blue eyes.

HEAD IN THE PASTEL CLOUDS

The album cover art let people know immediately that Taylor was in a new era. *Reputation* was dark, moody, and colorless. *Lover's* album art is completely different. It features lovely pastel clouds and a delicate font. Taylor has blue hair tips and a pink glittery heart around her right eye.

The press tour for Lover *was fun, light, and lovely.*

With her previous album, *Reputation*, Taylor avoided talking to the media. Though the album was very important to her, she feared that interviews would center on what she had gone through during that time in her life. She also didn't know what to say. "I couldn't figure out how I felt hour to hour," she later explained. *Lover* gave Taylor the freedom to focus solely on the music.

Lover was freeing in other ways too. It was Taylor's first album released with her new record label, Republic Records. This gave her more creative control. While *Lover* was mainly co-written and co-**produced** by Taylor and Jack Antonoff, Taylor also **collaborated** with other artists for the first time. Together, they created what Taylor described as "a love letter to love, in all of its maddening, passionate, exciting, enchanting, horrific, tragic, wonderful glory."

Taylor's Lover *performance looks were often bright and shiny.*

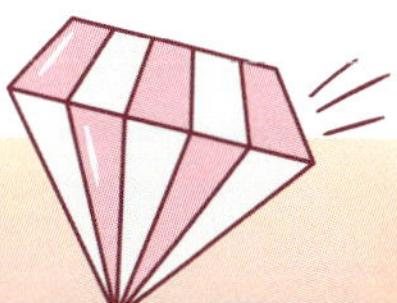

CHAPTER 3

BEHIND THE LYRICS

Like most of Taylor's albums, *Lover* reflects her personal life at the time it was written. *Reputation* helped Taylor break free from the people who wronged her. So, it was very fitting that the first track on her next album was "I Forgot That You Existed."

COMPLETE AN ACTIVITY HERE!

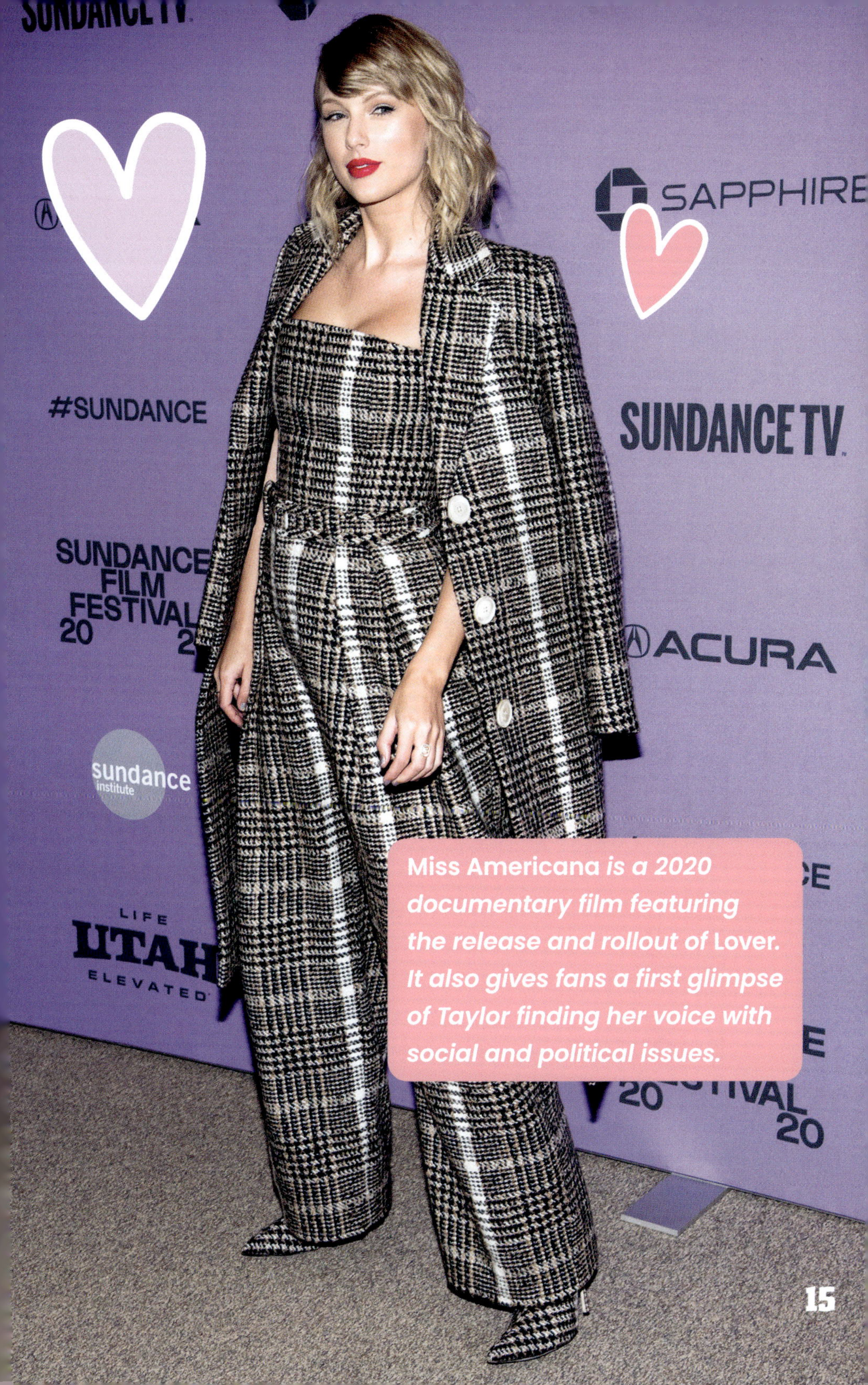

Miss Americana *is a 2020 documentary film featuring the release and rollout of* Lover. *It also gives fans a first glimpse of Taylor finding her voice with social and political issues.*

In line with "You Need to Calm Down," "Miss Americana & the Heartbreak Prince" is another song showing Taylor's willingness to speak out about her political beliefs. In the song, she uses high school social life and sports as **metaphors** for the state of American politics. For example, the lyrics "My team is losing / battered and bruising / I see the high fives between the bad guys / leave with my head hung / you are the only one who seems to care" show that Taylor was unhappy with the state of the country.

Taylor's Teen Choice Icon Award featured her three cats.

Remaining on theme, "The Man" examines the double standards that Taylor has faced as a successful female artist. She uses the lyrics to show how her life and career might have looked if she were a man.

Taylor wrote "Lover" for people to slow dance to. The first lyrics that came to her head were, "Can I go where you go? / Can we always be this close?" The **bridge** of the song, which begins "Ladies

Ballerina Misty Copeland (far right) danced for Taylor's performance of "Lover" at the 2019 American Music Awards.

and gentlemen, will you please stand?" is supposed to feel like wedding vows. Antonoff explained that the best feeling in the song is the transition from the bridge back to the chorus.

Taylor is known for being kind to her fans.

"Cruel Summer," which was released as a **single** in 2023, explores the highs and lows of a secret summer romance that leaves the narrator wanting something more. Taylor explained that the song has some of her favorite lyrics of the album. Her favorite line is "'I love you,' ain't that the worst thing you ever heard?"

The fifth track on the album, a spot often saved for Taylor's most **vulnerable** songs, is "The Archer." The song shows Taylor's awareness of her past mistakes and imperfections. The lyrics express how Taylor has been both the **instigator** (archer) and the victim (prey).

Taylor has always had to be fearless.

Easter Egg

The song title "The Archer" is a reference to Taylor's zodiac sign, Sagittarius. Sagittarians are often bold, fearless, and adventurous. They are also known to be great storytellers, just like Taylor!

CHAPTER 4

LOVER FEST

On September 17, 2019, Taylor announced Lover Fest. It would feature festival appearances and stadium shows in the United States and abroad. The tour was meant to kick off on April 5, 2020. But just before, the COVID-19 **pandemic** hit the

LEARN MORE HERE!

The only concert dedicated to Lover was City of Lover in Paris, France.

world. The tour dates were pushed further out but, in the end, Taylor had to cancel the tour completely.

Fans had to survive the next few years by rewatching *Lover* album music videos. All of Taylor's music videos are her vision, so her fans have fun finding all the Easter eggs she includes. In "The Man," there are two signs. One reads "Missing: If found return to Taylor Swift." The names of all of Taylor's albums surround it. The

other is a no scooters sign. Both refer to when record executive Scooter Braun purchased the rights to all of Taylor's music in 2019.

Taylor would later buy back all of her original music after lowering its value by re-recording each album.

The crowd erupted when Taylor made her grand entrance to kick off the Eras Tour show.

Luckily, *Lover* would get its time on tour. In March 2023, the much-anticipated Eras Tour kicked off. On night one, fans were excited to learn that Taylor devoted the first act to *Lover*. Taylor also chose to open the concert with "Miss Americana & the Heartbreak Prince." The lyric "It's been a long time coming" repeats before Taylor finally appears on stage.

Taylor's colorful *Lover* Era bodysuit called back to the album's cover art. Taylor wore it for every song in the set. However, she added a shiny, double-breasted blazer over the bodysuit to perform "The Man."

Lover was a new and exciting chapter in Taylor's career. It followed her *Reputation* Era, which was dark and more private. The *Lover* Era came with a clear change in how Taylor showed up in public. She was not afraid to speak her truth both personally and politically. Taylor explained, "It's so strange trying to be self-aware when you've been cast as this always smiling, always happy 'America's sweetheart' thing, and then having that taken away and realizing that it's actually a great thing that it was taken away, because that's extremely limiting."

The Lover House appeared during the Lover act of the Eras Tour. In the 1989 act, Taylor burned down the Lover House. This is meant to represent Taylor leaving the past behind.

The room colors in the Lover House represented each era of Taylor's career and life.

MAKING CONNECTIONS

TEXT-TO-SELF

What is your favorite song from the *Lover* Era? Why is it your favorite?

TEXT-TO-TEXT

Have you read books about any other music artists? How are they similar to or different from Taylor Swift?

TEXT-TO-WORLD

As a reader, why do you think so many people around the world connect with Taylor Swift and her music? Write a few sentences to explain your answer.

GLOSSARY

bridge — a section in the middle of a song that is clearly different from the other parts.

collaborate — to work with someone else on a project.

debut — to appear for the first time.

instigator — a person who purposefully starts drama or causes problems.

metaphor — a figure of speech in which a word or phrase is used in place of another to suggest a similarity in meaning between them.

optimistic — hopeful that things will work out well.

pandemic — an outbreak of a disease that spreads across a large area.

produce — to organize the creation of music recordings.

single — a song that is released as a stand-alone from the album.

studio — a place where recordings are made.

vulnerable — open to being hurt emotionally.

INDEX

DiscoverRoo!
ONLINE RESOURCES

This book is filled with videos, puzzles, games, and more! Scan the QR codes* while you read, or visit the website below to make this book pop.

popbooksonline.com/Lover

*Scanning QR codes requires a web-enabled smart device with a QR code reader app and a camera.